RAF
Colour Album

Compiled by
Malcolm English

Copyright © Jane's Publishing Company Limited 1986

First published in the United Kingdom in 1986 by
Jane's Publishing Company Limited
238 City Road, London EC1V 2PU

ISBN 0 7106 0204 9

Printed in the United Kingdom by
Netherwood Dalton & Co Ltd

JANE'S

Cover illustrations

Front: Pre-flight inspection of Lightning F6 XR759/AH of No 5
Squadron at RAF Binbridge in July 1983. It is camouflaged in three-
tone 'air superiority' grey and is carrying a pair of Red Top practice
missiles.

Rear: Lockheed Hercules C1 XV209 of No 30 Squadron based at
RAF Lyneham. Powered by four 4050 hp Allison turboprop
engines, the ubiquitous Hercules is used by No 30 Squadron to
provide tactical transport for both the RAF and Army. Two 5145
litre underwing drop tanks give it a range of 4250 nautical miles
which, while sufficient for most tasks, was inadequate for the long
flights to the Falkland Islands. To extend their range, aircraft were
fitted with an in-flight refuelling capability and some were converted
for a tanker role.

Right: Strapping in to Jaguar GR1 XZ117 of No 41 Squadron at
RAF Coltishall in July 1985. No 41 Squadron is tasked with tactical
strike and reconnaissance, for which it may be equipped with a
variety of conventional or nuclear stores, or an external
reconnaissance pod respectively.

For Aileen and Tracie

Introduction

The medium of colour photography provides an excellent opportunity to portray a wide variety of present day Royal Air Force aircraft types and to illustrate the many and varied roles undertaken by the Service at home and abroad.

In this book the fast jets such as the Tornado and Jaguar appear with their Support Command contemporaries like the TriStar and Hercules. Not forgotten, though, are earlier types operating in the latter years of their service lives, such as the Vulcan, Shackleton and Lightning.

Many ground and flight crews were introduced to flying and the Royal Air Force through Air Training Corps Air Experience flights and University Air Squadrons; their aircraft too are illustrated in this book.

Similarly, an immeasurable amount of interest in the Royal Air Force has been generated over the years by its aerobatic and display teams. What better examples than the Battle of Britain Memorial Flight, Vintage Pair and, of course, the Red Arrows?

While the Royal Air Force and industry have taken excellent photographs, the aim of this book is to provide as original a glimpse of the Service as possible. Therefore, I have used pictures from my own collection. I hope that they reflect my pride in the subjects and at least some of the enjoyment I experienced in photographing them.

Unfortunately, lack of space precludes personal acknowledgment to all those without whose assistance this book would not have been possible. To all Community Relations Officers, for their help and hospitality; ground and air crews, particularly those who patiently assisted in my air-to-air photographic sorties; and Strike and Support CPROs for granting facilities: please accept my grateful thanks.

Because of the high level of activity during which many of these photographs were taken it was not practicable to note exposure details. However, Kodachrome 64 film was used throughout, requiring a combination of 1/500th second at f5.6 to f8 for most of them. A pair of Olympus OM-1n cameras were used with Zuiko and Tamron lenses of 24mm, 50mm, 35–80mm zoom, 70–210mm zoom, 300mm and 500mm. All were fitted with UV filters.

T. MALCOLM ENGLISH BA, LRPS, MRAeS
September 1985

Left. Aptly named after the biblical 'mighty hunter', Nimrod MR2 XV237 of No 42 Squadron takes off with its four Rolls-Royce Spey turbofans at maximum power for the start of its display at the 1982 Battle of Britain Air Day, RAF Abingdon.

This self-portrait, taken over Anglesey during a training sortie from RAF Valley, in Summer 1985, illustrates the Hawk's excellent all-round field of view. The Hawk also has a roomy cockpit and low internal noise level which provides an ideal environment for instructor and pupil (or photographer).

Left. A red cross of Lorraine surmounted by a crown identifies this Jaguar T2A as an aircraft of No 41 Squadron. Armed with a practice bomb carrier on its centre line pylon, it was photographed taxiing past one of the RAF Coltishall hangars. No 41 Squadron is tasked with tactical strike and reconnaissance.

Above. Jaguar GR1 XX727 of No 54 Squadron was photographed in the company of a pair of Lightnings of No 11 Squadron during a refuelling exercise at 20,000 ft over the North Sea in June 1983. The Jaguar is equipped with a flight refuelling probe which is fully retractable. No 54 Squadron is one of three Jaguar units based at RAF Coltishall and received its first Jaguar in March 1974.

Below. Considering that all three of the Jaguar strike/reconnaissance squadrons are based at RAF Coltishall, it is somewhat surprising that the Jaguar Operational Conversion Unit is located at RAF Lossiemouth. 226 OCU aircraft may be recognised by the unit markings of shaft of arrows and beacon crossed and intertwined with a belt. The fin-mounted passive warning receiver and 'chisel nose' housing a laser ranger may be clearly seen in this view of XX766, pictured on take-off for its display at the 1980 RAF Alconbury Air Day.

Right. Numerically, the Jaguar has been the most important single aircraft in the RAF Germany inventory for many years, a situation that is only now changing with the advent of Tornado into service with RAF Germany. This picture of XZ382 of No 14 Squadron, RAF Brüggen, shows the protection afforded by the revetment surrounding the Jaguar's hardened aircraft shelter. In the event of the runway becoming unserviceable due to cratering, the Jaguar's levered-suspension enables it to land and take off from semi-prepared strips.

Engineers loading a 1000 lb practice bomb under the outer starboard underwing stores pylon of Jaguar GR1 XX970 of No 31 Squadron during Tactical Air Meet 1980 (TAM 80). The weapons normally carried by the Jaguar are 1000 lb iron bombs, BL755 cluster bombs or nuclear stores. The GR1 is equipped with two 30mm Aden guns housed in the fuselage and, as a result of Falklands and exercise experience, can carry AIM-9 Sidewinder missiles for self protection. Jaguars of No 31 Squadron gained full points in two of the events during TAM 80 and won the Broadhurst Trophy with maximum points in the low-level, shallow-angle bombing exercise. No 31 Squadron was converted to Tornadoes in early 1985.

Jaguar GR1 and T2s of No 2 Squadron serve with RAF Germany in the tactical reconnaissance role at RAF Laarbruch. The demanding reconnaissance task is eased by the Jaguar's navigation and weapon aiming sub-system which effectively replaces a navigator. Although not carried by XZ104, pictured here displaying at the 1980 Farnborough International Air Show, an external reconnaissance pod is normally fitted on the centreline pylon. Cameras with a range of focal length lenses to suit the task are installed in the pod. In addition, infra-red linescan is incorporated for poor weather or night missions.

Above. A sign at the gate of RAF Wittering proudly proclaims it to be the 'Home of the Harrier'. It is, in fact, the base of No 1 Squadron and the RAF's only Harrier training unit, namely 233 Operational Conversion Unit. There are two other Harrier Squadrons serving with RAF Germany. A detachment of No 1 Squadron is deployed to Belize as No 1417 Flight. This picture of Harrier GR3 XW769 of No 1 Squadron clearly shows the nose fairing housing a Ferranti Laser Rangefinder and Marked Target Seeker. A pair of eyelid shutters protect the lens when not in use.

Right. In its element, a Harrier GR3 of 233 OCU literally 'in the field' during an air display at the Shuttleworth Trust's airfield at Old Warden in July 1984. With the exception of the take-off and landing phases, the Harrier is considered to handle like any other high performance aircraft. Accordingly, training is very similar. Approximately six hours of helicopter experience is given the pilots passing through the OCU, to supplement some 21 Harrier sorties.

Although simple to fly and having a respectable weapon load/range for its size, it wasn't until it had proved itself in battle that the Harrier attained widespread credibility. In spite of its GR (ground attack and reconnaissance) designation the Harrier's ability to rapidly decelerate and/or change direction, using vectored thrust, together with its small size and smokeless engine make it a useful fighter. This photograph, taken in June 1981, shows a corner of the Engineering Wing's hangar at RAF Gütersloh, with Harriers of Nos 3 and 4 Squadrons in various maintenance states. Note the removable wings to facilitate engine changes.

Considering the Harrier's unique vertical take-off and landing capability, it seems paradoxical to house them in hardened aircraft shelters. At the first hint of an enemy attack this GR3 and the other aircraft of Nos 3 and 4 Squadrons, RAF Gütersloh, would deploy to pre-selected and prepared sites and melt into the countryside. As the nearest MiG-23 Flogger base is only 16 minutes flying time from RAF Gütersloh, the Harrier's V/STOL capability is ideally situated for the situation. This Harrier GR3 XV786 was photographed in June 1981.

13

Left. The Lightning first entered service on 29 June 1960 with No 74 Squadron and is still tasked with the primary role of United Kingdom Air Defence. Aircraft of Nos 5 and 11 Squadrons based at RAF Binbrook provide a quick reaction alert facility for the Southern UK region—a glowing testimony for an aircraft with over a quarter of a century of service. A Lightning F3 XR751 of the Lightning Training Flight, also based at RAF Binbrook, was photographed during a flying display at the 1980 RAF Alconbury Air Show. With their spectacular reheat climbs after take-off, Lightnings became one of the most popular display items on any air show programme.

Above. This Lightning F6 XR773 of No 5 Squadron was photographed being marshalled off the flight line at RAF Binbrook in June 1983.

The F6 was introduced in December 1965 to help resolve an endurance problem which had beset the Lightning throughout its formative years. This was achieved with the addition of a large ventral fuel tank, overwing 'ferry' tanks and an aerodynamically improved wing. The Lightning may be armed with either a pair of infra-red seeking Red Top or Firestreak missiles and the F6 carries a pair of 30mm Aden guns in the ventral tank.

As with all two-seat Lightnings, this T5 XS416 of the Lightning Training Flight has a full operational capability. Modelled on the single-seat F3, the most significant difference is the bulbous nose section to accommodate side-by-side seating. It was fortuitous that this configuration conforms well with area ruling—an aerodynamic design requirement for high-speed aircraft. This T5 is pictured carrying finless Red Top practice missiles.

Originally designed as a high altitude interceptor, the Lightnings are now usually to be found engaging targets at very low level. This change in operating environment has taken its toll of airframe fatigue life and was reflected, until recently, in their dark grey/green camouflage scheme. Even though Lightnings are still primarily operated in the low-level intercept role, they are now to be seen sporting two or three-tone 'air superiority' grey schemes. XS928, an F6 of No 11 Squadron was photographed in June 1983 at 20,000 ft over the North Sea, some 70 miles off Flamborough Head, while refuelling from a Vulcan K2.

Above. As a result of purchasing Phantom IIs for the Royal Navy and Air Force, two variants entered service at the end of the 1960s. A further variant, the F-4J (UK) was added to the inventory in July 1984 when No 74 Squadron was re-formed with the type. With the disbandment of 892 Squadron in December all of the Navy Phantoms, designated FG1, were adopted by the Royal Air Force who operated them alongside their FGR2s. No 92 Squadron is based at RAF Wildenrath but this FGR2 XV415 was pictured at the 1983 International Air Tattoo, Greenham Common.

Right. Phantom FGR2 XV412 of No 29 Squadron was photographed over the North Sea in March 1984. In addition to providing air defence of the United Kingdom, No 29 Squadron is assigned to Supreme Allied Commander Atlantic, tasked with air defence of maritime forces. During the Falklands Crisis, the squadron deployed firstly to Ascension Island to provide air defence of the staging base and sea routes and subsequently to RAF Stanley where it is responsible for the air defence of the Falkland Islands.

Left. This photograph of No 43 Squadron Phantom FG1 XV571/A and its crew at the 1984 RAF Wyton air day is typical of the many secondary tasks performed by both air and ground crew alike in 'showing the flag' at open days and air shows around the country.

Above. The Phantom Operational Conversion Unit, namely No 228 OCU, is based at RAF Coningsby where this FGR2 XV430 was photographed in February 1978. No 228 OCU aircraft wear the shadow squadron markings of No 64 Squadron, reflecting the unit's wartime role. All of the Phantoms are fully operational and would be manned in time of war by the unit's instructors, all of whom have front line squadron experience. It is interesting to note the absence of a passive radar warning receiver aerial fairing on the fin tip.

Despite the advent of air-to-air guided missiles as the primary fighter weapon, cannon remain a potent weapon for close-in combat. In order to remain proficient in air-to-air gunnery, air defence fighter squadrons of the Royal Air Force carry out a month of intensive gunnery training at RAF Akrotiri each year. Phantom FGR2 XV490 of No 56 'Firebird' Squadron is pictured taking-off from RAF Akrotiri in January 1985 for a sortie with a banner-towing Canberra. No 56 Squadron was formed in 1916 and soon attained fame when Captain Albert Ball shot down two enemy aircraft on the Squadron's first offensive patrol. It is now tasked with the air defence of the United Kingdom.

No 74 'Tiger' Squadron was re-formed in July 1984 at RAF Wattisham with F-4J (UK) Phantoms procured to rectify the shortfall in numbers of home-based air defence fighters resulting from the deployment of FGR2s to the Falklands. The F-4J (UK) differs from its FR1 and FGR2 counterparts primarily in having General Electric J-79 engines, and a missile control system which is on a par with F-14 Tomcat technology. Weapon loads are the same as the other air defence variants, namely four AIM-7 Sparrows plus four AIM-9L Sidewinders and a 20mm SUU-23A gun pod. The F-4Js will also be adapted to carry the Sky Flash radar homing missile. The camouflage was applied in the United States prior to delivery and is noticeably bluer than the standard 'air superiority' grey. This section of the No 74 Squadron flight line was photographed in September 1984.

Above. Originally built as a Canberra B4, WH876 was converted to a U10 and used as a target for missile trials. Having survived this ordeal, it was modified yet again into the mark in which it is pictured here, a U14. Now serving with the Aircraft & Armament Experimental Establishment, Boscombe Down, it must be sporting one of the most bizarre colour schemes worn by a Canberra. It was photographed at the International Air Tattoo, Greenham Common in May 1980.

Right. Two of the greatest problems of modern warfare is communications and weapon delivery in the presence of electronic countermeasures. Used successsfully they can render radar sets useless, radio communication impossible and even throw missiles off course. To provide NATO forces with experience of electronic warfare, No 360 Squadron operates Canberra T17s in an electronic countermeasures training role. WJ981 was operating out of its base at RAF Wyton when it was photographed from a Lightning T5 over the North Sea during an ECM training sortie in July 1983.

Left. No 1 Photo-Reconnaissance Unit was originally formed in 1939 with Spitfires and operated them until 1942, when the Unit was disbanded. Forty years later it was reformed at RAF Wyton where it now operates Canberra PR9s. The PR9 was designed to have an operating altitude of greater than 60,000 ft and accordingly features an increased wing area. Ironically, because of increased vulnerability at high altitude, the PR9s, along with all other strike aircraft in the RAF's inventory, are forced to operate at low level. Note the navigator's claustrophobic nose compartment.

Above. This fine study of Canberra T4 WJ879 belonging to No 231 OCU was taken on the approach to RAF Alconbury in July 1985, during a period in which 231's home base at RAF Wyton was undergoing runway resurfacing. In 1982 No 231 OCU celebrated its 30th year of continuous service with the same aircraft, a feat believed to be a British (if not world) record.

27

Above. Arguably the most graceful postwar fighter, the Hunter is considered by many who have flown it as THE pilot's aeroplane. The only RAF unit still to operate it is No 237 Operational Conversion Unit. A measure of the Hunter's success is the fact that it was flown by the air forces of some 19 countries. XL609, although in the colours of No 4 FTS, was photographed at RAF Honington in June 1980. It was based there to enable the Buccaneer crews maintain their flying hours while the Buccaneers were temporarily grounded due to fatigue problems.

Right. The crossed cutlasses and mortar board emblem on the nose of Hunter T7 WV322 identify it as belonging to 237 OCU. The task of this unit is to train pilots for the Buccaneer which, although a two-seat aircraft, has only one control column. There are no training versions of the Buccaneer, so students and converting pilots are given a few hours in the two-seat Hunters, some of which have representative instrument and control panels.

This view of Buccaneer XN981, taken from the back seat of another No 208 Squadron Buccaneer in September 1979, shows them out of their natural low-level environment. It was photographed at 15,000 ft en-route to the Tow Line 5 refuelling area over the North Sea. The zig-zag pattern in the cockpit canopy is miniature detonating cord which explodes and shatters the canopy when a crew member initiates ejection. This prevents injury during cockpit egress.

At the time of taking this photograph, in September 1979, No 208 Squadron was based at RAF Honington tasked with overland strike. In the summer of 1983 they moved to RAF Lossiemouth and now operate in the maritime strike and reconnaissance role. Optimised for high sub-sonic speed low-level flight, the Buccaneer's high wing loading gives the crew a smooth ride in the turbulent environment. However, XN981 is seen here a few minutes after the photograph on the opposite page was taken, refuelling from Victor K2 XL233 of No 55 Squadron at 15,000 ft.

In June 1926, No 12 Squadron was honoured by being equipped with Fairey Fox bombers, the only unit to fly the type. Hence was derived the squadron's badge of a fox's mask, and motto, 'leads the field'. XV359 is pictured taxiing at RAF Akrotiri in January 1984 where it was operating in support of the British Forces in Lebanon. Note the AN/ALQ101 jamming pod mounted on the underwing pylon, which reduces the Buccaneer's vulnerability to enemy defences. Aircraft from Nos 12 and 208 Squadrons were flown in support of the British Forces in Lebanon during 1983-84, for which they were also equipped with chaff and flare dispensers, and Paveway/Pavespike laser guided bomb units.

This scene at RAF Laarbruch is typical of the toned down airfields of RAF Germany on which there is a distinctly different atmosphere to those in the United Kingdom. A No 16 Squadron Buccaneer S2 is pictured taxiing out of its har-dened aircraft shelter in June 1981. The Buccaneer S2 has a total store load of 7257 kg which it can carry in its novel rotating bomb bay and on four underwing stores pylons. In addition to four wing stations, which can carry defensive weapons such as an AIM-9 Sidewinder and/or electronic countermeasure pod, a pair of slipper tanks containing 1136 litres each may be fitted.

Left. Tornado is destined to be the backbone of Western European air power into the 21st century with a total number of 644 GR.1s scheduled to enter service with the Royal Air Force, German Air Force, German Navy and Italian Air Force. To minimise training costs to these three nations, the Tri-National Tornado Training Establishment was formed at RAF Cottesmore. With 50 aircraft on strength of the TTTE, all pilots and navigators are trained to a common standard. ZA356 is a dual control version of the GR1, designated GR1T and was pictured on approach to RAF Coltishall in March 1985, where it was serving with C Squadron.

Below. The Greek letter Beta identifies this TTTE Tornado GR1T as an aircraft of B Squadron. ZA324 is pictured during a 'touch and go' at RAF Cottesmore in June 1985. Both RB199s are in reheat and the undercarriage has almost retracted. Out of the total of 50 aircraft on the strength of the TTTE, 21 are British.

Left. Justification for including this and the picture below in a book on the Royal Air Force is that although they carry the colours of Germany and Italy, they are flown by pilots and navigators of different nationalities. It is the TTTE policy for aircraft of whatever country to be manned by crews of different nationalities. Pictured on the approach to RAF Cottesmore, 43+12 of A Squadron, was illuminated from below by reflections off snow-covered fields in March 1985.

Left. In addition to its three basic training squadrons the TTTE also has a Standards Squadron. This is responsible for advanced training, instructor training and special duties. The markings of the Standards Squadron are a letter S pierced with a sword. I-44 was pictured at RAF Cottesmore in June 1985. There are seven Italian aircraft on the strength of the TTTE and an Italian Officer commands C Squadron. A Squadron is commanded by a German and B Squadron by a Briton.

This Tornado GR1 of No 15 Squadron was photographed as it taxied out of its hardened aircraft shelter at RAF Laarbruch. No 15 Squadron was the first RAF Germany unit to receive the type. ZA447 was pictured on a rainy day in September 1984, the sort of day which is ideal for the Tornado with its terrain following radar and ground mapping radar. Typical weapon loads for the Tornado GR1 include JP233 runway denial weapons, cluster weapons and conventional bombs. The aircraft also has a nuclear strike capability.

This No 617 Squadron aircraft, seen festooned with warning pennants, was photographed in its hardened shelter at RAF Marham in July 1985.

The lightning flash, just discernible on the fuselage badge, symbolises the breaching of the Ruhr dams.

One of four Tornado GR1s of No 27 Squadron arriving at RAF Akrotiri in January 1984 en-route to Oman for exercise Magic Carpet. Possibly as a result of this deployment, during which they carried out in-theatre training and joint exercises with the Sultan of Oman's Air Force, the Sultan has ordered a number of Tornado F2s.

Developed from the Tornado GR1 to provide a high performance interceptor with long range, the F2 retains much of the GR1's structure. The most significant change is the addition of a lengthened nose section to house the Foxhunter radar, although this first prototype, ZA254, lacked a radar fit, being an aerodynamic trials vehicle. Photographed at the 1980 Farnborough Air Show, it was displayed with four dummy Sky Flash air-to-air missiles in recesses under the belly.

Tornado F2s are in service with No 229 Operational Conversion Unit at RAF Coningsby where ZD906 was pictured in July 1985, taxiing out of a hardened aircraft shelter. Currently armed with Sky Flash air-to-air missiles, it will later be equipped with AMRAAM (advanced medium range air-to-air missiles). Sidewinders are carried for shorter range engagements and a 27mm Mauser cannon is fitted for very short range combat.

This view of Hawker Siddeley Nimrod MR2 XV245 illustrates the close resemblance to the de Havilland Comet on which the design was based. The most obvious external differences are the Magnetic Anomaly Detector boom extending aft of the fuselage and the hemp camouflage scheme. Internally, the MR 2 carries a multitude of sensors to enable it to locate surface ships and submarines. Armament includes up to nine torpedoes as well as bombs in an unpressurised bomb bay, and underwing hardpoints for the carriage of air-to-surface or air-to-air missiles. XV245 is in operation with No 42 Squadron, based at RAF St. Mawgan. Since this photograph was taken in September 1982, the aircraft has been fitted with an in-flight refuelling probe.

A view of the flight deck of Nimrod MR1 XV244 on the return, off-task, to its home base of RAF St. Mawgan during exercise Ocean Safari in June 1983. Ocean Safari is a major, annual maritime/air exercise designed to test procedures and the protection of shipping against attack from submarines, warships and aircraft. In this particular exercise, more than 90 ships and submarines, including four aircraft carriers, and some 300 aircraft were involved. Participating aircraft included Shackleton AEW2s, Buccaneers, Canberra T17s, E3A Sentry AWACS, Auroras and Atlantics. XV244 has since been modified to MR 2 standard with improved communications and sensor equipment.

The first aircraft to become embroiled in the Falklands conflict were a pair of Nimrods based at Wideawake, tasked with providing a 400 mile surveillance around the Falklands. Aircraft serving in the South Atlantic were rapidly equipped with 'strap-on goodies' including a flight refuelling probe and underwing missile rails. XV234 was photographed at Wideawake airfield in August 1982 shortly after the cessation of hostilities.

Nimrod MR2s are in service with Nos 42, 120, 201 and 206 Squadrons, plus 236 OCU, which are situated logically at the northern and southern bases of Kinloss and St. Mawgan. They are tasked primarily with the demanding cat and mouse game of anti-submarine warfare, often flying 12-hour sorties. Typically the Nimrod cruises on three engines until its weight reduces to 65,770 kg when a second engine may be shut down. XV258 was photographed on the approach to RAF Mildenhall in June 1984; note the large flaps.

Shackleton AEW2s are in service with No 8 Squadron, RAF Lossiemouth, where this photograph of engineers working on a propeller assembly was taken in May 1982. Described as 10,000 rivets flying in close formation, the Shackleton was derived from a maritime reconnaissance version of the famous Lancaster bomber.

The latest development of the Nimrod is the AEW3 variant. To provide optimum radar coverage without interference from the fuselage, the radar scanners have been mounted at the extremities of the fuselage. As a result, the overall length is 3·34 m greater than the MR1 model on which it is based. Similarly, the wingspan has been increased slightly, with the addition of wingtip sensor pods. A total of 11 AEW3s were scheduled to be fully operational with No 8 Squadron at RAF Waddington in 1985 but major problems with the radar system are causing a slippage. XZ286 was the first aerodynamically representative AEW3 airframe and was pictured two months after its first flight at the 1980 Farnborough International Air Show.

Left. Although no longer in service, the Avro Vulcan was given a short, last minute reprieve in the spring of 1982. With the outbreak of hostilities in the South Atlantic, crews from disbanded Vulcan squadrons were hastily reformed to fly radar suppression and bombing missions against the Argentine forces in the Falklands. For increased protection against defences on the Island, the Vulcan's electronic countermeasure equipment was supplemented by external jamming pods. XM575 of No 44 Squadron was photographed 'over the moon' in June 1982 during a display at RAF Mildenhall.

Above. The Vulcan's farewell: a pair of Vulcan K2s of No 50 Squadron photographed during a sortie to mark the retirement of the last Vulcans from operational service, on 30 March 1984.

49

Prior to providing in-flight refuelling support for aircraft operating 'down South', the original task of Handley Page Victors from Nos 55 and 57 Squadrons and No 232 OCU was maritime radar reconnaissance of the area around the Falkland Islands. XL163 of No 57 Squadron was pictured at Wideawake airfield in August 1982, sporting the Squadron's new fin markings — a phoenix arising from a fire.

Victor K2 XL188 of No 55 Squadron was photographed in the latest hemp camouflage scheme at the 1985 International Air Tattoo, RAF Fairford. Although trailing three drogues, it is usual practice to refuel only one or two aircraft at a time from the underwing pods, or a single aircraft from the centre hose drum unit. This is because of limited wingspan clearance between the receivers.

Left. In order to airlift materials and personnel the 3400 nautical miles from Ascension Island to the Falklands, the Hercules' normal 2500 nautical mile range was extended by fitting long-range fuel tanks and an in-flight refuelling capability. C1K tanker Hercules were flown by crews of Nos 47 and 70 Squadrons, RAF Lyneham, and the C1 and C3 transports by crews of Nos 24 and 30 Squadrons, also from RAF Lyneham. A complex refuelling technique known as a toboggan manoeuvre was developed to enable the Hercules to be refuelled in flight from the higher speed Victor tankers. Hercules C1K XV213 of 1312 Flight RAF Stanley is pictured trailing its refuelling drogue at the 1985 International Air Tattoo, RAF Fairford.

Above. Hercules C1K XV204 of 1312 Flight RAF Stanley is pictured taxiing from the flight line at Wideawake airfield in August 1982.

53

In addition to the long-range fuel tanks, refuelling probes and hose drum units fitted to many of the Hercules fleet during the Falklands conflict by Marshall of Cambridge, the Company have also been contracted to convert 30 aircraft to C3 standard. Basically this involves adding two fuselage barrel sections giving a total length increase of 4·57 m. An example of one of the modified aircraft is XV188, pictured here landing at RAF Akrotiri in January 1984.

This Hercules W2 must be one of the strangest sights in the sky around the Royal Aircraft Establishment, Farnborough, where it is currently in service with the Meteorological Research Flight. XV208 is the sole W2 in existence and was photographed during a flying display at the RAF Mildenhall Air Fete in June 1984. The long nose probe contains vanes and pressure sensors to measure turbulence ahead of the aircraft outside of its pressure field, and the large pylon-mounted fairing above the cockpit contains a weather radar.

Left. Two BAe 146 C Mk 1s have been assessed by No 241 Operational Conversion Unit, RAF Brize Norton, for acquisition by the Queen's Flight. ZD696, civilian serial G-SSCH, was photographed in July 1983 while serving with the OCU but has since been returned to the manufacturer pending the arrival of two new machines. In its civilian role, the BAe 146 Series 100 is capable of carrying up to 93 economy class passengers; needless to say, there will be fewer occupants in the Queen's Flight aircraft!

Above. No 32 Squadron, based at RAF Northolt received its first BAe 125 in March 1971 and now has three variants of the type in service — CC1, CC2 and CC3. Originally powered by Rolls-Royce Viper turbojet engines, the CC1 and CC2 models have all been re-engined with more economical and quieter turbofans. Externally the CC1 and CC2 variants may be differentiated by the number of cabin windows, the former having five and the latter six. XX508 was photographed in February 1985 while refuelling, prior hangared for the night.

XS794 is an Andover CC2 on the strength of No 32 Squadron, based at RAF Northolt and tasked with VIP duties. The Squadron's badge, a hunting horn stringed, may be seen above the aircraft's fin flash. It is seen here in front of one of the Northolt hangars, prior to a night sortie in February 1985.

A flagship of the Royal Air Force, this Andover CC2 of the Queen's Flight based at RAF Benson must be one of the most immaculate aircraft in service. A member of the crew is pictured polishing a propeller blade during a visit to RAF Finningley by Princess Ann in May 1985. XS789 is one of three Andover CC2s in service with the Queen's Flight.

No 60 Squadron was re-formed at RAF Wilden-rath, Germany, in February 1969, with Hunting Pembroke C Mk 1s operating in the light transport and communications role, a task they continue to this day. A re-sparring programme performed by BAe some years ago extended the fleet life considerably.

This pair of de Havilland Devon C Mk 2s of No 207 Squadron was photographed during a four-ship formation in June 1984 to mark the Squadron's imminent disbandment. As the Southern Communications Squadron, No 207 had operated Devons since its formation in February 1969. It is understood that the aircraft are to be offered for sale on the open market.

Above. The VC10 C Mk 1, with its side-loading cargo door and in-flight refuelling capability, remains the principal strategic transport aircraft. During the Falklands conflict the VC10s, which are in service with No 10 Squadron, Brize Norton, performed stirling service transporting personnel and materials from bases in the United Kingdom to Ascension Island, and evacuating the sick and wounded back home. A total of 125 passengers may be accommodated for scheduled flights, or up to 150 troops; alter-natively a maximum of 78 stretchers or nine stretchers and 61 seated casualties, or assorted freight loads up to a maximum of 24,494 kg may be carried. XV107 was photographed during the RAF Abingdon Battle of Britain Air Display, September 1982.

Right. No 101 Squadron officially reformed with VC10 K Mk 2 tankers on 1 May 1984 at RAF Brize Norton and received the first of its K Mk 3s the following year. Its primary role is the refuelling support of air defence fighters. Equipped with two underwing hose drum units and a third in the rear fuselage, the tankers are able to transfer up to 165,000 lb (K Mk 2) and 187,000 lb (K Mk 3) at a rate of approximately 4000 lb/min. Refuelling operations are moni-tored on the flight deck by means of a remotely-controlled TV camera which provides a visual display for the Flight Engineer. ZA140 was photographed over Cornwall in March 1984 from another VC10 K Mk 2.

The first of six Lockheed L-1011-500 TriStar K1 tankers for the RAF ZD950 was photographed at the 1985 International Air Tattoo, RAF Fairford, whose theme was Sky Tanker '85. The largest aircraft in RAF service, the TriStars are powered by three 222·4 kN Rolls-Royce RB211 turbofans.

A total of six British Airways and Pan American TriStar Series 500 aircraft have been procured by the RAF for service with No 216 Squadron, based at Brize Norton. Initially operating in the passenger and cargo transport role, the TriStars will ultimately become multi-role aircraft with a tanking capability. With a capacity for 330 passengers it is expected to be used primarily for the South Atlantic run to RAF Stanley. ZD952, ex-G-BFCE, was photographed at RAF Akrotiri in January 1984.

Above. Gazelle HT3 XW855 is pictured in the neat grey and white colours of No 32 Squadron. Photographed at its home base of RAF Northolt in January 1985, this squadron is tasked with communications and VIP executive duties.

Gazelle HCC4s are also operated by the squadron for its executive flights. An excellent safety feature of the Gazelle is its shrouded tail rotor. *Right.* Gazelle HT3s are in service with the helicopter element of the Central Flying School,

based at RAF Shawbury. The sleek HT3 is a vast improvement in terms of speed and range performance over its predecessor, the Bell 47 Sioux. XW898 of No 2 Flying Training School was photographed at Biggin Hill in May 1978.

The Boeing Vertol Chinook was designed to meet a 1959 US Army requirement for a medium transport helicopter capable of carrying an internal load of two tons (2032 kg). Powered by two 3750 shp Avco Lycoming engines the HC1, which is in service with Nos 7 and 18 Squadrons and No 240 OCU, can carry over 6000 kg. ZA673/FG is on the strength of No 18 Squadron, based at RAF Gütersloh, which is tasked with logistic support of the BAOR. It was photographed in May 1982 at the Biggin Hill Air Fair. Three of No 18 Squadron's Chinooks were lost with the sinking of the support ship *Atlantic Conveyor* during the Falklands conflict.

Helicopters have added a new dimension to modern warfare, from the gunships in Vietnam to the Sea King HAR2 AEW of the Falklands conflict. On a more passive note, the rescue helicopters operating in the South Atlantic undoubtedly prevented countless injured from becoming fatalities. Chinooks from Nos 7 and 18 Squadron were deployed from their bases at Odiham and Gütersloh during 1983-84 to support the British Forces in Lebanon. This photograph was taken in January 1984 at RAF Akrotiri where the Chinooks were based.

Above. There are two overseas Wessex units, namely Nos 84 and 28 Squadrons, in Cyprus and Hong Kong respectively. Both are equipped with Wessex HC2s for tactical support duties. XV719 of No 84 Squadron was photographed at Dhekelia in January 1984. No 84 Squadron is normally tasked with supporting the British and the United Nations Forces in Cyprus from its base at RAF Akrotiri. When this picture was taken it was also involved with ferrying supplies to the British forces in Lebanon.

Right. XV732 is, without a doubt, one of the smartest Wessex helicopters in service, the other is its sister Wessex HCC4 in service with the Queen's Flight at RAF Benson. Apart from the immaculate red and royal blue colour scheme, in common with the Queen's Flight Andovers, the HCC4 may be identified by folding steps below the cabin door. Both Prince Philip and Prince Charles are current on the Queen's flight aircraft. XV732 was photographed at RAF Coltishall in July 1985.

Left. All RAF search and rescue aircrews receive their training at the Search and Rescue Training Unit, based at RAF Valley. Equipped with four Westland Wessex HAR2s, the unit passes out 160 students a year. In addition to being a training unit, SARTU also assists at rescues if C Flight of No 22 Squadron, which is also resident at RAF Valley, is away. Since its arrival at RAF Valley in 1955, No 22 Squadron has flown on over 3000 rescue missions. XT601 was photographed during a training sortie with the SARTU in July 1985.

Above. Royal Air Force helicopters tasked with search and rescue duties are conventionally painted a high-visibility yellow colour scheme. The dark sea grey of this Westland Sea King HAR3 is a relic of its Falklands duties. ZA105 is assigned to No 202 Squadron which has detachments at RAF Boulmer, Brawdy, Coltishall, Lossiemouth and Stanley. With a true all-weather capability, the HAR3 can pick up 18 survivors out to its operating radius of 280 nautical miles.

73

No 33 Squadron has performed in a wide variety of roles since its formation in 1916. Initially a home defence fighter squadron, it then flew bombers until receiving Gladiators in 1938 when it became a fighter squadron, a role it retained until its disbandment in 1962. From 1965 until 1970 it was based in Malaysia as a Bloodhound air defence squadron, reforming in 1971 at Odiham with Puma HC1s, tasked with tactical support. Pumas also serve with No 230 Squadron, Gütersloh, 1563 Flight, Belize, and 240 Operational Conversion Unit. XW236 of No 33 Squadron, was photographed while on fire duty at the Farnborough International Air Show, 1980.

Bristol Bloodhound Mk 2s of B Flight No 25 Squadron, photographed at RAF Wyton in July 1985. RAF Wyton is also the headquarters of No 25 Squadron, with A and C detached Flights at RAF Barkston Heath and Wattisham respectively. The Bloodhound originally entered service to counter high-altitude attacks but is now tasked primarily with low-level defence.

Left. It would be an understatement to say that by modern standards the Slingsby Grasshopper T Mk 1 primary glider is 'basic'. Nevertheless, some 60 of this type are still in service with Combined Cadet Forces (RAF) throughout the country, providing cadets with an understanding of flight. WZ827 was photographed outside the flight hangar at RAF Syerston in June 1985.

Above. The Schleicher ASK 21 Vanguard T Mk 1 was one of the first glassfibre gliders to enter service with the Air Cadet organisation. This one was photographed in October 1984 at the start of an air-tow from RAF Syerston. There are ten of these two-seat high-performance gliders operated by 618 Volunteer Gliding School, West Malling and the Air Cadet Central Gliding School, Syerston.

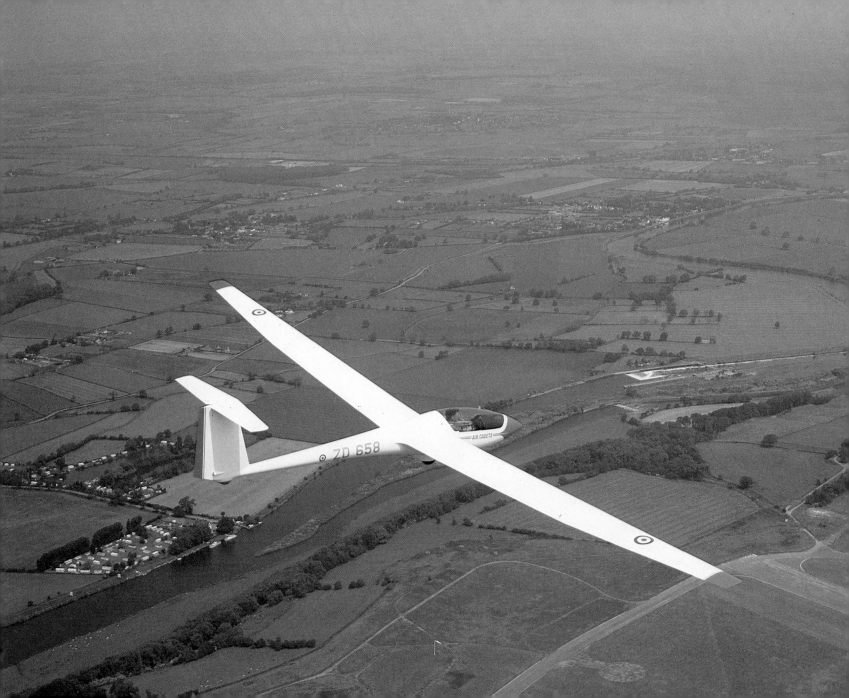

Left. A Schleicher AWS 19 Valiant T Mk 1 over the Syerston runway, June 1985. Five Valiant T Mk 1 single-seat high-performance gliders entered service during 1983, primarily to give instructors advanced experience. They also enable specially selected cadets to receive advanced glider training. The Valiant is of a sufficiently high performance to enable the Air Cadet organisation to confidently compete in national glider championships for the first time since 1967.

Above. With the advent of the RAF's long-grass policy to deter birds from nesting on airfields, the ability of the Slingsby Venture Mk 2 to operate off runways is invaluable. Winch-launched gliders are flown from grass strips adjacent to runways. The self-launch capability of the Venture, afforded by its Rollason-Volkswagen 1600 cc engine, has minimised the ground support required and its longer flight duration enables instruction to be more concentrated. With power off the glide performance is equal to that of the Sedbergh. A cadet is pictured being given a pre-flight briefing prior to a dual sortie from RAF Syerston, June 1985.

Above. Chipmunk T Mk 10 WZ856 is operated by No 7 Air Experience Flight based at RAF Newton near Nottingham, hence the Robin Hood symbol in the Flight's crest. The AEF's catchment area includes East Midlands Wing, Lincolnshire/South Humberside Wing and 65 per cent of South Midlands Wing. It also flies cadets from 14 Combined Cadet Force (RAF) units and provides glider towing support for RAF Syerston.

Right. Chipmunk T Mk 10s are in service with twelve of the thirteen Cadet Air Experience Flights in the United Kingdom. The AEFs were formed in 1958 with a nucleus of 50 surplus Chipmunks made available by the closure of the Royal Air Force Volunteer Reserve. They are tasked with flying all Air Training Corps cadets who have passed their first class cadet examination, to give them at least 25 minutes of flying time per year. WP970 is on the strength of No 5 AEF, Cambridge. Formed in July 1958 at Marshall's airfield at Cambridge, the Flight serves the ATC Squadrons in nine counties as well as 19 Combined Cadet Force (RAF) school units.

University Air Squadrons were introduced just after the First World War at the instigation of Lord Trenchard to encourage an interest in flying and promoting and maintaining liaison with the Universities in technical and research problems affecting aviation. The Cambridge UAS came into existence on 1 October 1925, becoming in the process the first squadron of its kind anywhere in the world. A further milestone in the UAS's history was the acceptance of female members in 1985-1986. BAe Bulldog XX634 is operated by Cambridge UAS, one of the 16 Squadrons in the United Kingdom, and was photographed in June 1985.

This Beagle Husky was originally a raffle prize in aid of mentally handicapped children, won by Mr Fred Pontin. It was subsequently bought by Mr Bobby Butlin who then presented it to the Air Training Corps in 1969. Operated by No 5 AEF from their base at Cambridge, where it was photographed in June 1985. It has the advantage of accommodating three cadets as compared to the Chipmunk's one.

Above. Jet Provost T Mk 3As are in operation with three Flying Training Schools. This particular aircraft XM352, photographed at the International Air Tattoo, Greenham Common, in June 1981 was in service with No 7 FTS at RAF Church Fenton.

Right. This T Mk 5 XW309 of No 6 Flying Training School was photographed during a low-level navigation exercise through the Lake District from its base at RAF Finningley. The Jet Provost T Mk 5 entered service with the RAF in 1961 and is now only flown by No 6 FTS

who use it to introduce navigation students to the fast jet cockpit environment. Compared to the other Jet Provost variants still in service, the T Mk 5 has the advantage of higher thrust than the T Mk 3A and greater endurance than the T Mk 5A.

Above. Currently in service with the Brazilian Air Force, the Shorts/EMBRAER Tucano (Tucan) won the competition for a future RAF basic training aircraft required to replace the Jet Provost fleet. Other short-listed contenders were the British Aerospace/Pilatus PC-9, Hunting Firecracker and the Australian AAC/Westland A.20. PP-ZTC was photographed at the Farnborough Air Show, September 1984. The flame underneath the flaps is issuing from an underwing smoke generator used during the Tucano's display.

Right. The BAe Hawk entered service in 1976 and is now operating from two RAF training units, RAF Valley and the Central Flying School headquarters, Scampton. XX223 is on the strength of the CFS at RAF Valley and was photographed over the base during a training sortie in July 1985. The CFS is tasked with training Hawk instructors and providing refresher and fast jet orientation courses. Powered by a Rolls-Royce Turboméca turbofan rated at 23·13 kN, the Hawk has a maximum level speed of 535 kts/Mach 0·87 and handling characteristics which have been described as ideal for an advanced trainer — brisk, yet docile.

The Hawk is a sufficiently manoeuvrable air-craft to peform a useful air defence role in war-time. Accordingly, the RAF has equipped a large percentage of them with the capability of carrying AIM-9 Sidewinder heat-seeking mis-siles on underwing pylons. They will primarily be used to supplement Phantom and Lightning air defence forces and may operate as a mixed formation. The wide performance range of such a defence would pose quite a problem to an attacking force. Hawk TMk 1A XX339 of No 234 shadow Squadron, No 1 Tactical Weapons Unit was photographed during its display at the Old Warden Military Air Pageant, July 1985.

XX343 is one of three Hawk T Mk 1s to be operated by the Empire Test Pilots School at the Aeroplane & Armament Experimental Establishment, Boscombe Down. One of the School's other Hawks, XX343 is currently being equipped with a variable stability flying control system at the College of Aeronautics, Cranfield. The ETPS was established in 1943 to train test pilots. It is now equipped with a wide range of aircraft including Lightning, Hunter and Andover in addition to rotary wing types such as the Lynx, Gazelle and Sea King. Among the unique instrumentation fit is a voice warning system. This features the voice of actress Norma Ronald passing advice to the pilot. The ultimate message he could receive would be 'if not recovered — eject!'

Above. Designed and manufactured by Handley Page, the T Mk 1 is the military version of the Jetstream Series 200 civil passenger aircraft. They are currently operated by the Multi Engine Training Squadron of No 6 Flying Training School, based at RAF Finningley. As the name of the Squadron implies, the Jetstreams are used to train and refresh pilots essentially for the maritime, transport and tanker forces. Sorties are flown up to 25,000 ft and the training syllabus includes a flight to West Berlin.

Right. The Dominie T1 is a military development of the Hawker Siddeley HS 125 executive jet, and is in service with No 6 Flying Training Squadron, based at RAF Finningley primarily to train navigators. Navigators destined for fast jet squadrons complete a course on the Dominie prior to flying in the Jet Provost. It is now also used for the flying training of Air Electronic Operators and Air Engineers. The three aircraft pictured here were photographed over the Humber bridge during a formation practice sortie by the Operations and Pilot Training Wing, Standards Squadron.

The Meteor represents important milestones in the history of the Royal Air Force. A Meteor 1 was the first jet aircraft to enter service with the Royal Air Force and the T7 formed the mainstay of advanced jet training in the 1950s and 1960s.

It is appropriate that this Meteor T7 WA669 is based at the headquarters of the Central Flying School, RAF Scampton. Flown by CFS instructors, WA669 forms half of the Royal Air Force's Vintage Pair display team.

Vampire T11 XH304 is the other half of the Vintage Pair and represents the type which became the first jet trainer to serve the Royal Air Force College, Cranwell. It is an interesting foil to the Meteor in having only one engine and side by side seating. XH304 was photographed over the Yorkshire moors on a sortie from the Pair's previous base at RAF Leeming in April 1984.

Left. The Battle of Britain Flight was formed at RAF Biggin Hill in 1957 to commemorate the Service's major battle honour and to serve as a reminder of the vital role played by the Royal Air Force in the defence of the country. Now based at RAF Coningsby, the Lancaster, Spitfires and Hurricanes of the Flight still evoke nostalgia at their many air display appearances. Lancaster PA474 is pictured with the serial letters AJ-G, which was the code carried by Wing Comman-der Guy Gibson, VC when leading No 617 Squadron on the Möhne dams raid. For the 1985 display season it was painted in the markings of an aircraft of No 101 Squadron, SR-D.

Left. Hurricanes were responsible for 60 percent of the enemy aircraft brought down during the Battle of Britain, and are represented by LF363 and PZ865. This photograph of Hurricane IIc LF363 was taken during a display at the 1985 RAF Mildenhall Air Fete. It depicts the black colour scheme and coding, VY-X, of a No 85 Squadron aircraft while it was engaged in the night fighter role.

Above. Spitfire Mk Vb AB910 was built in 1941 at Castle Bromwich and saw service during the war. On 4 August, 1945 an ACW 2 Margaret Horton was holding the tailplane down for an engine run, in a similar manner as the groundcrewman in this photograph, when the pilot, Flight Lieutenant Cox — who thought that she had got off — took off and flew a circuit, wondering why the tail was reluctant to come up! She was unhurt and visited the flight in 1968. Marked XT-M, the aircraft was pictured in No 603 Squadron letters at the 1982 Mildenhall Air Fete.

Tailpiece: the Red Arrows were formed in 1965 with the Folland Gnat, converting in 1980 to the BAe Hawk. The Red Arrows are not an elite group, but represent a typical cross section of squadron pilots and ground crew, epitomising the skill and dedication demanded and achieved by the Royal Air Force.